THE ULTIMATE MEDITERRANEAN DIET COOKBOOK FOR BEGINNERS 2023

2000+ Days of Easy Recipes to Lose Weight While Savoring Your Favorite Foods | 30-Day No-Stress Meal Plan for Eating Well Every Day

Taylor Molina

Table of Contents

INTRODUCTION 1

CHAPTER 1: HOW TO GET STARTED WITH MEDITERRANEAN DIET? 3

    Your goals 3

    Pick a date 3

    Take the first step 3

    Clean your pantry 3

    Make the transition 4

    Support system 4

    Be patient 4

SHOPPING LIST 5

TRICKS AND TIPS THAT WILL MAKE THINGS EASIER 6

THREE REASONS WHY YOU ARE NOT LOSING WEIGHT IN THE MEDITERRANEAN DIET 7

    Calories 7

    You're concentrating on diet and ignoring exercise. 7

    You're eating prematurely rather than savoring your meal. 7

CHAPTER 2: BREAKFAST RECIPES 8

RECIPE 1: ARTICHOKE FRITTATA 8

RECIPE 2: AVOCADO BAKED EGGS 9

Recipe 3:	Buttery Pancakes	10
Recipe 4:	Cheesy Green Bites	12
Recipe 5:	Heavenly Egg Bake with Blackberry	14
Recipe 6:	Omelet	16
Recipe 7:	Nectarin Bruschetta	18
Recipe 8:	Poached Eggs with Avocado Puree	19
Recipe 9:	Stuffed Pita Breads	20
Recipe 10:	Tuna Breakfast Quiche	21
Chapter 3:	**Beans, Grains, and Pasta Recipes**	**22**
Recipe 11:	Asparagus Risotto	22
Recipe 12:	Brown Rice Pilaf with Pistachios and Raisins	23
Recipe 13:	Chicken Curry Rice	24
Recipe 14:	Mushroom Risotto	25
Recipe 15:	Turkey Pasta Toss	26
Chapter 4:	**Vegetable Main Recipes**	**27**
Recipe 16:	Artichokes Provencal	27
Recipe 17:	Cauliflower Curry	29
Recipe 18:	Eggplant Ratatouille	30
Recipe 19:	Veggie Quesadillas	32
Recipe 20:	Zucchini Lasagna Rolls	33

CHAPTER 5: FISH AND SEAFOOD RECIPES 35

RECIPE 21: BROILED SALMON 35

RECIPE 22: HALIBUT WITH KALE 36

RECIPE 23: SEAFOOD GUMBO 37

RECIPE 24: SHRIMP ZOODLES 39

RECIPE 25: TILAPIA 40

CHAPTER 6: POULTRY AND MEAT RECIPES 41

RECIPE 26: ARTICHOKE BEEF ROAST 41

RECIPE 27: CHICKEN AND ARTICHOKES 43

RECIPE 28: GROUND PORK SKILLET 44

RECIPE 29: HERB AND PISTACHIO TURKEY BREASTS 46

RECIPE 30: POT-ROAST VEAL 47

CHAPTER 7: SIDES, SALADS AND SOUP RECIPES 48

RECIPE 31: BAKED TOMATO 48

RECIPE 32: BALSAMIC BEETS 49

RECIPE 33: CARROT AND BROCCOLI SALAD 50

RECIPE 34: CHICKEN KALE WRAPS 51

RECIPE 35: CREAMY CARROT CHOWDER 52

RECIPE 36: CRISPY SWEET POTATO FRIES 53

RECIPE 37: ENDIVE SALAD 54

RECIPE 38:	LEEKS SOUP	55
RECIPE 39:	MUSHROOM SPINACH SOUP	56
RECIPE 40:	WHITE BEAN AND KALE SOUP WITH CHICKEN	57
CHAPTER 8:	DESSERT RECIPES	58
RECIPE 41:	BLUEBERRY MUFFINS	58
RECIPE 42:	CHERRY CLAFOUTIS	60
RECIPE 43:	CITRUS CIAMBELLA	61
RECIPE 44:	COCOA BROWNIES	62
RECIPE 45:	FIG AND HONEY BUCKWHEAT PUDDING	63
RECIPE 46:	MAPLE BAKED PEARS	64
RECIPE 47:	ROSE CRÈME CARAMEL	65
RECIPE 48:	SPANISH NOUGAT	66
RECIPE 49:	VANILLA BREAD PUDDING WITH APRICOTS	67
RECIPE 50:	WHITE CHOCOLATE BRIE CUPS	69
CHAPTER 9:	30-DAY MEAL PLAN	70
CONCLUSION		73

Introduction

The Mediterranean diet claims, shedding a lot of fat and relaxing will keep you healthy. If you want to shed weight and keep it off, the Mediterranean way of life is the solution you've been waiting for. This diet reflects a different way of life. You'll want to hear more about the Mediterranean diet in the long term.

It is a basic diet. The Mediterranean diet takes a very direct approach. Naturally, France and Italy have had a major impact on the Mediterranean diet. A low incidence of heart disease was found in men who lived in Crete, one of the regions where the Mediterranean diet was first used, according to several medical studies. In other studies, a Mediterranean diet has also been linked to a reduced risk of stroke and hypertension-related death. It was discovered that following this diet helped avoid skin wrinkling and decreased skin cancer in those who adopted it. This diet is also helpful to the lungs, as it decreases the risk of clogged arteries, which everyone is afraid of.

Start with a Mediterranean diet if you want to be as safe as possible. Sunlight is helpful to one's wellbeing. A healthy lifestyle is beneficial to your well-being. A healthy way of living enhances a good life. Your health will benefit from a Mediterranean diet. It is a smart thing to employ a physical strategy to accomplish the objective of getting cured.

When the Mediterranean diet was first discussed publicly in the United States in the 1970s, it referred to a form of cooking that was both healthy and tasty. It's worth noting that the Mediterranean diet was not created to prevent heart disease. It was developed due to the advent of human heart disease. This diet was developed by people who had no idea what heart disease was and didn't feel they were coping. It was set up on very large farms with fields, orchards, vineyards, walnut groves, and olive groves on them. They processed their meat and dairy. They grew their crops and consumed very little wheat. They ate a wide range of meats, including lamb, goat, turkey, and pork. Basic spices were also used to flavor the food. The more cooked and processed foods were consumed, the more people developed illnesses linked to eating too much of them.

The primitive Mediterranean diet was discovered to be one of the best, if not the best, diet that was available, and it was much superior to modern diets.

The Mediterranean diet has been extensively researched. It has been tested from every possible perspective and confirmed to be the safest diet on the planet. It's easy to follow and doesn't necessitate any special cooking methods or nutritionist assistance.

How to Get Started with Mediterranean Diet?

Your goals

Before starting this diet, spend some time and develop the goals you wish to achieve.

Pick a date

Once you know your goal, you should work on setting a timeline. Select a date you want to start this diet. Don't be in a rush, and don't think you can get started with this diet right away. It takes a while to prepare your mind and body for the diet you wish to follow. The Mediterranean diet doesn't require any drastic dietary changes. However, if your diet is rich in processed foods and sugars, your body will take time to adjust to the new diet. Therefore, pick a date and ensure you start your diet on that particular date. Don't make any excuses, and don't try to put it off until a later date. If you keep telling yourself that you can start this diet tomorrow, then tomorrow will never come. Take a calendar, mark the date, and get started.

Take the first step

Once you have made up your mind about this diet, then it is time to get started. Don't get scared of the diet; instead, think of it as a stepping-stone towards better health. If you get scared, remind yourself of the goals you wish to achieve from this diet.

Clean your pantry

It's time to go grocery shopping after you've made this list. Simultaneously, you're also supposed to eliminate any other items that don't fit the Mediterranean diet eating protocols. As a result, it's essential to eliminate all processed meals, bad carbohydrates, and sugary sweets from your diet. Think of it as a kitchen spring cleaning. It is quintessential that you do this because if you're surrounded by temptations all the time, the chances of giving in to your urges to eat unhealthy foods will increase.

Make the transition

Once you follow the steps mentioned up until now, it is time to make the transition. As mentioned in the previous point, if your diet is predominantly rich in processed foods and sugars, it might be a little tricky to shift to any other diet. You might not know this, but a diet rich in sugars is quite addictive to your body. You can either go cold turkey or make a slow transition to the new diet. Slowly start eliminating all unhealthy foods from your diet while incorporating Mediterranean diet-friendly foods. This way, you are conditioning your mind and body to get used to the new diet. Give yourself two to three weeks to consider this diet before deciding.

Support system

If you want to adhere to this diet in the long term, you'll need a support structure. Let go of the mindset of "I'll simply wing it." There will be days when you don't feel motivated. Here's where your support system comes in. Whenever you feel like you don't have the motivation to keep going, you can depend on your support system. Your support system can include your partner, loved ones, friends, or anyone else you want. Talk to them about your reasons for following the diet and tell them what you wish to achieve. You are making yourself responsible to someone else by doing so. This, in turn, increases your motivation to stick to this diet. You can always get online and get in touch with those following the same diet as you.

Be patient

A common mistake a lot of dieters make is that they are always in a hurry. Not just time, but consistency as well. Don't think that you'll be able to shed all those extra pounds overnight. Therefore, you can't expect yourself to get rid of it quickly. Whenever you make a dietary change, you might notice certain fluctuations in your energy levels. Take it easy if you can't work out as hard as you used to. Within two to three weeks, your energy levels will stabilize, your body will get used to the new diet, and you will be able to exercise the way you want. Until then, be patient and don't weigh yourself daily. It might be quite tempting to see whether you've lost any weight daily, but it is not practical. On certain days, the scale will not move as much as you would want. Make weighing oneself at least once a week a habit. It will help you monitor your development.

Shopping List

Use this basic shopping list whenever you shop for groceries. Ensure that you stock your pantry with all these ingredients and get rid of any other item, which is not suitable for your diet. Your shopping list must include:

- Veggies like kale, garlic, spinach, arugula, onions, carrots
- Fruits like grapes, oranges, apples, and bananas
- Berries like blueberries, strawberries, raspberries
- Frozen veggies
- Grains like whole-grain pasta, whole-grain breads
- Legumes like beans, lentils, chickpeas
- Nuts like walnuts, cashews, almonds
- Seeds like pumpkin seeds and sunflower seeds
- Condiments like turmeric, cinnamon, salt, pepper
- Shrimp and shellfish
- Fish like mackerel, trout, tuna, salmon, and sardines
- Cheese, Yogurt, and Greek yogurt
- Potatoes and sweet potatoes
- Chicken
- Eggs
- Olives
- Olive oil and avocado oil

If you buy healthy and adequate ingredients, you will certainly eat the right foods and stay on your diet.

Tricks And Tips That Will Make Things Easier

- Keeping in mind that you cannot eat red meat, you can replace it with salmon.
- If you are on the Mediterranean diet, you must forget about using butter, but you can replace it with extra virgin olive oil.
- Give up consuming sodas and replace them with some red wine. Cut out the sweet drinks from your diet and try one glass of red wine instead.
- Replace white rice with brown rice. The Mediterranean diet allows you to continue to eat rice but make sure you replace the white rice with a brown one. Consume whole grains like buckwheat, corn, and quinoa.
- Your snacks should mainly contain fruits. Consume more citrus, melons, berries, or grapes. You can also try seeds as a Mediterranean diet snack, but fruits would be a better option.
- Another great idea to keep in mind when you are on such a diet is to make a great shopping list like the one above. Choose organic products if you can, but only if they suit your budget.
- You must keep your body hydrated. Regardless of the dietary changes you make, you must always concentrate on proper hydration. When your body is hydrated, all the toxins present within will be flushed out. Also, when you're transitioning to this diet or making any dietary changes, hunger pangs are quite common.

Three Reasons Why You Are Not Losing Weight in The Mediterranean Diet

Before you dive into a Week Meal Plan, let's briefly look at some of the reasons why you might not be losing weight even if you are on a Mediterranean Diet.

Calories

Suppose you don't spend your entire day performing physical labor or are a dynamic athlete. In that case, you almost certainly won't lose weight eating 2,000 calories each day unless you incorporate exercise into the routine. Likewise, simply walking up several flights of stairs to your workplace won't burn enough calories to qualify as a good workout. Many people overestimate the calories they burn per day normally by as much as 25%. Keep track and make use of a journal or an app.

You're concentrating on diet and ignoring exercise.

The Mediterranean diet is more than a shopping list and a cookbook. Though it is possible to lose excess weight by modifying diet alone, it is difficult to do it with a sedentary lifestyle. Adding regular physical exercise to any weight loss regimen increases your likelihood of burning more calories than you consume, causing you to slim down even more consistently. To make the Mediterranean diet a highly effective weight loss strategy, make sure to keep the body moving.

You're eating prematurely rather than savoring your meal.

Spend time looking for fresh ingredients, cooking with friends or family, and lingering at the table to enjoy your dinner.

To be sure you're not overcooking it, pre-portion your nut products in plastic bags or reusable containers to be sure you can enjoy the health advantages without accidentally consuming more than you designed to.

Breakfast Recipes

Artichoke Frittata

Serving Size: 4

Cooking Time: 10 minutes

Ingredients:

- 8 large eggs
- ¼ cup of Asiago cheese, grated
- 1 tablespoon of fresh basil, chopped
- 1 teaspoon of fresh oregano, chopped
- Pinch of salt
- 1 teaspoon of extra virgin olive oil
- 1 teaspoon of garlic, minced
- 1 cup of canned artichokes, drained
- 1 tomato, chopped

Directions:

1. Pre-heat your oven to broil. Take a medium bowl and whisk eggs, Asiago cheese, oregano, basil, sea salt, and pepper.
2. Oil and heat the pan and add the garlic plus the egg mixture. Return skillet to heat and sprinkle artichoke hearts and tomato over eggs.
3. Cook frittata without stirring for 8 minutes. Broil skillet for 1 minute until lightly browned. Cut frittata into 4 pieces and serve. Enjoy!

Nutritional Value: Calories 199; Fat 13g; Carbohydrates 5g; Protein 16g

Avocado Baked Eggs

Serving Size: 2

Cooking Time: 25 minutes

Ingredients:

- 2 eggs
- 1 medium sized avocado, halved and pit removed
- ¼ cup cheddar cheese, shredded
- Kosher salt and black pepper, to taste

Directions:

1. Mix the egg and avocado season with black pepper and salt.
2. Top with cheddar cheese and transfer the muffin pan in the oven.
3. Bake for about 15 minutes and dish out to serve.

Nutritional Value: Calories 210; Fat 16.6g; Carbohydrates 6.4g; Protein 10.7g

Buttery Pancakes

Serving Size: 5

Cooking Time: 10 minutes

Ingredients:

- 1 cup wheat flour, whole-grain
- 1 teaspoon baking powder
- 1 teaspoon lemon juice
- 3 eggs, beaten
- ¼ cup Splenda
- 1 teaspoon vanilla extract
- 1/3 cup blueberries
- 1 tablespoon olive oil
- 1 teaspoon butter
- 1/3 cup milk

Directions:

1. In the mixer bowl, combine together baking powder, wheat flour, lemon juice, eggs, Splenda, vanilla extract, milk, and olive oil.
2. Blend the liquid until it is smooth and homogenous.
3. After this, toss the butter in the skillet and melt it.
4. With the help of the ladle pour the pancake batter in the hot skillet and flatten it in the shape of the pancake.
5. Sprinkle the pancake with the blueberries gently and cook for 1.5 minutes over the medium heat.
6. Repeat the same steps with all remaining batter and blueberries.
7. Transfer the cooked pancakes in the serving plate.

Nutritional Value: Calories 152; Fat 7.5g; Carbohydrates 30.6g; Protein 7.4g

Cheesy Green Bites

Serving Size: 8

Cooking Time: 15 minutes

Ingredients:

- ¼ cup frozen chopped kale
- ¼ cup finely chopped artichoke hearts
- ¼ cup ricotta cheese
- 2 tablespoons grated Parmesan cheese
- ¼ cup Goat cheese
- 1 large egg white
- 1 teaspoon dried basil
- 1 lemon, zested
- ½ teaspoon salt
- ½ teaspoon freshly ground black pepper
- 4 frozen filo dough, thawed
- 1 tablespoon extra-virgin olive oil

Directions:

1. Combine kale, artichoke, ricotta, Parmesan, Goat cheese, egg white, basil, lemon zest, salt, and pepper in a bowl. Place a filo dough on a clean flat surface. Brush with olive oil.
2. Place a second filo sheet on the first and brush with more oil. Continue layering to form a pile of four oiled sheets. Working from the short side, cut the phyllo sheets into 8 strips and half them.
3. Spoon 1 tablespoon of filling onto one short end of every strip.

4. Repeat the process with the other filo bites. Place a trivet into the pot. Pour in 1 cup of water. Cook for 15 minutes and serve.

Nutritional Value: Calories 326; Fat 25g; Carbohydrates 38g; Protein 13.3g

Heavenly Egg Bake with Blackberry

Serving Size: 4

Cooking Time: 15 minutes

Ingredients:

- Chopped rosemary
- 1 teaspoon lime zest
- ½ teaspoon salt
- ¼ teaspoon vanilla extract, unsweetened
- 1 teaspoon grated ginger
- 3 tablespoon coconut flour
- 1 tablespoon unsalted butter
- 5 organic eggs
- 1 tablespoon olive oil
- ½ cup fresh blackberries
- Black pepper to taste

Directions:

1. Blend all the ingredients reserving the berries and pulse for 2 to 3 minutes until well blended and smooth.
2. Take four silicon muffin cups, grease them with oil, evenly distribute the blended batter in the cups, top with black pepper and bake for 15 minutes until cooked through and the top has golden brown.
3. When done, let blueberry egg bake cool in the muffin cups for 5 minutes, then take them out, cool them on a wire rack and then serve.
4. For meal prepping, wrap each egg bake with aluminum foil and freeze for up to 3 days.

5. When ready to eat, reheat blueberry egg bake in the microwave and then serve.

Nutritional Value: Calories 144; Fat 10g; Carbohydrates 2g; Protein 8.5g

Omelet

Serving Size: 4

Cooking Time: 15 minutes

Ingredients:

- 1 garlic clove
- 4 large eggs, beaten
- 2 tablespoons chopped fresh parsley
- 1/4 cup thinly sliced red onion
- 2 teaspoons extra-virgin olive oil
- 2 tablespoons chopped fresh basil
- 1/2 teaspoon salt
- 1/2 yellow bell pepper
- 1/2 teaspoon black pepper
- 1/2 red bell pepper

Directions:

1. In a big heavy pan, heat 1 teaspoon olive oil. Cook the peppers, garlic, and onion in the pan for 5 minutes.
2. Add the basil, parsley, salt, and pepper and cook for 2 minutes. Return the pan to heat after removing the vegetable mixture to a dish.
3. Pour the beaten eggs into the hot 1 teaspoon olive oil, stirring to coat evenly. 3–5 minutes, or until the rims are boiling and the eggs are dry except for the middle.
4. To turn the omelet over, either flip it or use a spatula.
5. Spoon the vegetable mixture over one-half of the omelet and fold the empty side over the top with a spatula. Place the omelet on a cutting board or a plate.

6. Serve.

Nutritional Value: Calories 197; Fat 18g; Carbohydrates 41g; Protein 6g

Nectarin Bruschetta

Serving Size: 2

Cooking Time: 15 minutes

Ingredients:

- 1 ½ tablespoon of white wine vinegar
- 1 teaspoon of honey
- 1 nectarine, sliced
- ¼ cup of olive oil
- 2 teaspoons of black pepper
- ⅓ cup of fresh ricotta cheese
- 2 slices of bread, toasted

Directions:

1. Mix the teaspoon of honey and the tablespoon of white wine vinegar in a medium-sized bowl. Stir in the sliced nectarine, mix it well and marinate for approximately about 10 minutes.
2. Add the black pepper and olive oil, then mix well. Spread the cup of fresh ricotta cheese over the slices of toasted bread. Divide the nectarine and its juice on top of the bread. Serve.

Nutritional Value: Calories 247; Fat 29.1g; Carbohydrates 18.5g; Protein 6.4g

Poached Eggs with Avocado Puree

Serving Size: 4

Cooking Time: 5 minutes

Ingredients:

- 2 avocados, peeled and pitted
- 1/4 cup chopped fresh basil leaves
- 3 tablespoons red wine vinegar
- Juice of 1 lemon
- Zest of 1 lemon
- 1 garlic clove, minced
- 1 teaspoon sea salt
- 1/8 teaspoon freshly ground black pepper
- Pinch cayenne pepper, plus more as needed
- 4 eggs

Directions:

1. Combine the avocados, basil, 2 tablespoons vinegar, lemon juice and zest, garlic, 1/2 teaspoon salt, pepper, and cayenne in a blender. Purée for 1 minute, or until completely smooth.
2. Pour approximately three-quarters of a cup of water into a 12-inch nonstick pan and set it over medium heat. Add the remaining 1/2 teaspoon sea salt and 1/4 cup vinegar.
3. Crack the eggs carefully into the custard cups. Carefully slide the eggs into the simmering water, one at a time, while holding the cups slightly above the water. Wait 5 minutes without stirring or raising the lid.
4. Place each egg on a dish and drizzle with the avocado purée.

Nutritional Value: Calories 213; Fat 20g; Carbohydrates 11g; Protein 2g

Stuffed Pita Breads

Serving Size: 4

Cooking Time: 15 minutes

Ingredients:

- 1 and ½ tablespoons olive oil
- 1 tomato, cubed
- 1 garlic clove, minced
- 1 red onion, chopped
- ¼ cup parsley, chopped
- 15 ounces canned fava beans, drained and rinsed
- ¼ cup lemon juice
- Salt and black pepper to the taste
- 4 whole-wheat pita bread pockets

Directions:

1. In a medium-hot pan, heat the oil and sauté the onion for 5 minutes.
2. Stir in the other ingredients and simmer for another 10 minutes.
3. Serve the pita pockets stuffed with this mixture for breakfast.

Nutritional Value: Calories 382; Fat 1.8g; Carbohydrates 66g; Protein 28.5g

Tuna Breakfast Quiche

Serving Size: 4

Cooking Time: 30 minutes

Ingredients:

- 3 eggs
- 3 tablespoons of oats
- 3 tablespoons of cream cheese
- 1 tablespoon of dill
- 1 tablespoon of basil
- 1 cup of can tuna, drained
- ½ onion, chopped
- ½ carrot, grated
- ½ zucchini, grated
- Salt and pepper

Directions:

1. Preheat the oven to 350° F. In a bowl, whisk eggs with cream cheese, pepper, and salt.
2. Bake the egg mixture for 20 minutes. Allow to cool then slice and serve.

Nutritional Value: Calories 151; Fat 6.6g; Carbohydrates 6.4g; Protein 16.4g

Beans, Grains, and Pasta Recipes

Asparagus Risotto

Serving Size: 4

Cooking Time: 30 minutes

Ingredients:

- 5 cups vegetable broth
- 3 tablespoons unsalted butter
- 1 tablespoon olive oil
- 1 small onion, chopped
- 1½ cups Arborio rice
- 1-pound fresh asparagus
- ¼ cup of Parmesan cheese, grated, plus more for serving

Directions:

1. Boil the vegetable broth. Reduce to low heat and maintain the broth at a constant simmer.
2. Oil and heat the pan with onions plus the rice.
3. Stir in ½ cup of warm broth. Cook, often stirring, for about 5 minutes until the broth is completely absorbed.
4. Add the asparagus stalks and another ½ cup of broth. Cook, often stirring until the liquid is absorbed. Continue adding the broth, ½ cup at a time, and cooking until it is completely absorbed before adding the next ½ cup. Stir frequently to prevent sticking. The rice should be cooked yet firm after approximately 20 minutes.
5. Serve and enjoy.

Nutritional Value: Calories 434; Fat 14g; Carbohydrates 13g; Protein 10g

Brown Rice Pilaf with Pistachios and Raisins

Serving Size: 6

Cooking Time: 20 minutes

Ingredients:

- 1 tablespoon extra-virgin olive oil
- 1 cup chopped onion
- ½ cup shredded carrot
- ½ teaspoon ground cinnamon
- 1 teaspoon ground cumin
- 2 cups brown rice
- 1¾ cups pure orange juice
- ¼ cup water
- ½ cup shelled pistachios
- 1 cup golden raisins
- ½ cup chopped fresh chives

Directions:

1. Oil and heat the pan with onion. Add the carrots, cinnamon, and cumin, cook until aromatic.
2. Pour into the orange juice, brown rice, and water. Bring to a boil.
3. Transfer the rice mixture in a large serving bowl, then spread with pistachios, raisins, and chives.
4. Serve immediately.

Nutritional Value: Calories 264; Fat 7.1g; Carbohydrates 48.9g; Protein 5.2g

Chicken Curry Rice

Serving Size: 5

Cooking Time: 1 hour 25 minutes

Ingredients:

- 1 tablespoon curry paste
- ¼ cup milk
- 1 cup wheatberries
- ½ cup of rice
- 1 teaspoon salt
- 4 tablespoons olive oil
- 6 cups chicken stock

Directions:

1. Place the chicken broth and wheat berries in the pan, cook for 60 minutes.
2. After the time is up, add the rice, olive oil, and salt, and mix well.
3. In a bowl, mix the milk, and curry paste, then add the liquid into the rice mixture, and mix well. Cook for 15 minutes.
4. Serve.

Nutritional Value: Calories 232; Fat 15g; Carbohydrates 23.5g; Protein 3.9g

Mushroom Risotto

Serving Size: 4

Cooking Time: 3 hours 30 minutes

Ingredients:

- 1 onion, chopped
- 1 teaspoon of olive oil
- 9 ounces of chestnut mushrooms, sliced
- 4 cups of vegetable stock
- 1 3/4 ounces of porcini
- 10 ½ ounces of wholegrain rice
- Small bunch of parsley, chopped
- Grated parmesan cheese, to serve

Directions:

1. Sauté the onion in a skillet with oil for 10 minutes.
2. Stir in the mushroom slices and cook until soft.
3. Pour the stock and porcini then let it simmer.
4. Remove and set aside for 5-10 minutes to soak.
5. Add the mushrooms, porcini, stock and onions to a slow cooker.
6. Cook for 3 hours on high with rice.
7. Garnish with parsley and parmesan. Serve warm.

Nutritional Value: Calories 363; Fat 3.8g; Carbohydrates 76.9g; Protein 17g

Turkey Pasta Toss

Serving Size: 6

Cooking Time: 15 minutes

Ingredients:

- 3 cups uncooked penne pasta
- 2 Italian turkey sausage links, casings removed
- 1 large sweet yellow pepper, strips
- 1 tbsp. olive oil
- 6 garlic cloves, minced
- 4 plum tomatoes, cut into 1-inch chunks
- 20 pitted ripe olives, halved
- 1/4 cup minced fresh basil
- 1/4 tsp. crushed red pepper flakes
- 1/4 tsp. salt
- 1/4 cup shredded Romano cheese

Directions:

1. Cook the pasta following the package instructions. In the meantime, cook and crumble sausage in a big skillet on medium heat until the meat is not pink anymore; drain, then keep warm.
2. Sauté pepper in the same pan with oil until tender-crisp; put in the garlic. Cook for another minute. Mix in sausage, tomatoes, salt, olives, pepper flakes, and basil. Drain the pasta, then mix into the skillet; thoroughly heat. Top with sprinkled cheese.

Nutritional Value: Calories 292; Fat 15g; Carbohydrates 17g; Protein 16g

Vegetable Main Recipes

Artichokes Provencal

Serving Size: 4

Cooking Time: 25 minutes

Ingredients:

- ½ of a medium white onion chopped
- 2 medium tomatoes
- 18 ounces frozen artichoke hearts
- 1 teaspoon minced garlic
- ¾ teaspoon salt
- ½ teaspoon ground black pepper
- 1 tablespoon olive oil
- ½ cup white wine
- ½ teaspoon lemon zest
- 3 tablespoons water

Directions:

1. Place a medium skillet pan over medium heat, add oil, add onion, garlic, and ¼ teaspoon salt when hot.
2. Cook for just about 5 minutes or until softened, stir in wine, and cook for 3 minutes or reduce by half.
3. Add tomatoes, artichoke hearts, salt, lemon zest, and water and continue cooking for 6 minutes, covering the pan and stirring occasionally.

4. Season with rest of the remaining salt and black pepper, add basil and olives and cook for 1 minute.
5. Remove pan from heat and serve straightaway.

Nutritional Value: Calories 200; Fat 16g; Carbohydrates 40g; Protein 15g

Cauliflower Curry

Serving Size: 4

Cooking Time: 35 minutes

Ingredients:

- 2 tablespoons of olive oil
- ½ cauliflower, chopped into florets
- ¼ teaspoon of salt
- 1 teaspoon of curry paste
- 1 cup of unsweetened coconut milk
- ¼ cup of fresh cilantro, chopped
- 1 tablespoon of lime juice

Directions:

1. Oil and heat the pan with cauliflower for 10 minutes.
2. Mix the coconut milk and curry powder, add to the cauliflower, and simmer for ten minutes.
3. Add the cilantro and lime juice.
4. Serve and enjoy!

Nutritional Value: Calories 243; Fat 24g; Carbohydrates 9g; Protein 3g

Eggplant Ratatouille

Serving Size: 2

Cooking Time: 15 minutes

Ingredients:

- 1 eggplant
- 1 sweet yellow pepper
- 3 cherry tomatoes
- 1/3 white onion, chopped
- 1/2 teaspoon garlic clove, sliced
- 1 teaspoon olive oil
- 1/2 teaspoon ground black pepper
- 1/2 teaspoon Italian seasoning

Directions:

1. Preheat the air fryer to 360 F.
2. Peel the eggplants and chop them.
3. Put the chopped eggplants in the air fryer basket.
4. Place the cherry tomatoes in the air fryer basket.
5. Then add olive oil, sliced garlic clove, chopped onion, ground black pepper, and Italian seasoning.
6. Chop the sweet yellow pepper roughly and add it to the air fryer basket.
7. Shake the vegetables gently and cook for 15 minutes.
8. Stir the meal after 8 minutes of cooking.
9. Transfer the cooked ratatouille to the serving plates.
10. Enjoy!

Nutritional Value: Calories 249; Fat 3.7g; Carbohydrates 28.9g; Protein 5.1g

Veggie Quesadillas

Serving Size: 3

Cooking Time: 4 minutes

Ingredients:

- 1 cup black beans, cooked
- ½ red bell pepper, chopped
- 4 tablespoons cilantro, chopped
- ½ cup corn
- 1 cup low-fat cheddar, shredded
- 6 whole-wheat tortillas
- 1 carrot, shredded
- 1 small jalapeno pepper, chopped
- 1 cup non-fat yogurt
- Juice of ½ lime

Directions:

1. Spread half of the tortillas with the black beans, red bell pepper, 2 tablespoons cilantro, corn, carrot, jalapeño, and cheese, then top with the other half of the tortillas.
2. Cook for 3 minutes on one side, flip, and cook for 1 more minute on the other side before transferring to a dish. 3.
3. Repeat the process with the remaining quesadillas.
4. Mix 2 tablespoons of cilantro, yogurt, and lime juice in a small bowl until thoroughly combined. Serve with the quesadillas.
5. Enjoy!

Nutritional Value: Calories 200; Fat 3g; Carbohydrates 13g; Protein 7g

Zucchini Lasagna Rolls

Serving Size: 4

Cooking Time: 50 minutes

Ingredients:

- 10 oz package frozen spinach, thawed and squeezed dry
- 1 large egg
- 2 large zucchini trimmed
- 1 1/3 cup part-skim ricotta
- 8 tablespoons shredded smoked mozzarella cheese
- 1 minced garlic clove
- 2 tablespoons chopped fresh basil
- ¾ cup low sodium marinara sauce
- 3 tablespoons grated Parmesan cheese
- ¼ teaspoon salt
- ½ teaspoon ground pepper
- 2 teaspoons extra-virgin oil

Directions:

1. Slice the zucchini lengthwise, 1/8-inch thick each, to get a total of 24 strips. In a large bowl, toss the zucchini in oil, 1/8 teaspoon of salt, and ¼ teaspoon of pepper. Arrange the zucchini on the prepared pans. Bake the zucchini for about 10 minutes or till it becomes tender.
2. Mix 2 tablespoons of mozzarella and 1 tablespoon of Parmesan cheese. Set aside, and in a medium bowl, mix the egg, spinach, ricotta, garlic, and the remaining 2 tablespoons of Parmesan, 6 tablespoons of mozzarella, 1/8 teaspoon of salt, and ¼ teaspoon of pepper.

3. Set a spoonful of the ricotta mixture at the bottom of each zucchini strip, wrap it up, and place it in the baking dish seam-side down.
4. Bake the zucchini rolls till they are lightly browned on top. Allow standing for 5 minutes, then sprinkle with basil before serving.

Nutritional Value: Calories 315; Fat 18.6g; Carbohydrates 16.8g; Protein 22g

Fish and Seafood Recipes

Broiled Salmon

Serving Size: 4

Cooking Time: 20 minutes

Ingredients:

- 4 fillet salmon
- 1 tablespoon chopped fresh cilantro
- 4 pressed garlic cloves
- ½ cup olive oil
- ¼ cup balsamic vinegar
- 1 ½ teaspoon garlic salt
- 1 tablespoon chopped fresh basil

Directions:

1. A little bowl with olive oil and balsamic vinegar. Grease a baking dish and place the salmon on it. Rub garlic on the salmon fillets, then pour the vinegar-oil mixture over them, turning once to coat. Season with salt, basil, and cilantro. Set aside to marinate for 10 minutes
2. Preheat the oven's broiler to 450°F/230°C.
3. Place the salmon approximately 6 inches from the heat source until it is browned on both sides and flakes easily with your fingers.

Nutritional Value: Calories 390; Fat 5.4g; Carbohydrates 3.6g; Protein 15g

Halibut with Kale

Serving Size: 4

Cooking Time: 25 minutes

Ingredients:

- 3 tablespoons of olive oil, divided
- 3 cups of kale, coarsely chopped
- 2 cups of cherry tomatoes, halved
- 4 (4-ounce) boneless, skinless halibut fillets
- Juice and zest of 1 lemon
- Sea salt and black pepper, to taste
- 1 tablespoon of fresh basil, chopped

Directions:

1. Preheat the oven to 375°F.
2. Lightly grease an 8x8" baking dish with two teaspoons of olive oil.
3. Drizzle over the rest of the remaining olive oil and the lemon juice, lemon zest, basil, salt, and pepper. Bake until the bunch of fish flakes easily and the greens are wilted (about 15 minutes).
4. Serve and enjoy.

Nutritional Value: Calories 228; Fat 10g; Carbohydrates 9g; Protein 28g

Seafood Gumbo

Serving Size: 4

Cooking Time: 30 minutes

Ingredients:

- ¼ cup tapioca flour
- ¼ cup olive oil
- 1 cup celery, chopped
- 1 white onion, chopped
- 1 red bell pepper, chopped
- 1 green bell pepper, chopped
- 1 red chili, chopped
- 2 cups okra, chopped
- 2 garlic cloves, minced
- 1 cup canned tomatoes, crushed
- 1 teaspoon thyme, dried
- 2 cups fish stock
- 1 bay leaf
- 16 ounces canned crab meat, drained
- 1-pound shrimp, peeled and deveined
- ¼ cup parsley, chopped
- Salt and black pepper to the taste

Directions:

1. Oil and heat the pan, add the flour, whisk to obtain a paste, and cook for about 5 minutes.
2. Add the bell peppers, the onions, celery, and the okra and sauté for 5 minutes.

3. Stir in the other ingredients (except the crab, shrimp, and parsley), reduce to low heat, and cook for 15 minutes.
4. Add the remaining ingredients, simmer the soup for 10 minutes more, divide into bowls and serve.

Nutritional Value: Calories 363; Fat 2g; Carbohydrates 18g; Protein 40g

Shrimp Zoodles

Serving Size: 2

Cooking Time: 10 minutes

Ingredients:

- 2 zucchini, spiralized
- 1 lb shrimp, peeled and deveined
- 1/2 teaspoon paprika
- 1 tablespoon basil, chopped
- 1/2 lemon juice
- 1 teaspoon garlic, minced
- 2 tablespoon olive oil
- 1 cup vegetable stock
- Pepper
- Salt

Directions:

1. Oil and heat the pot, Add garlic and sauté for a minute.
2. Add shrimp and lemon juice and stir well and cook for 1 minute.
3. Add remaining ingredients and stir well.
4. Once done, release pressure using quick release. Remove lid.
5. Serve and enjoy.

Nutritional Value: Calories 215; Fat 9.2g; Carbohydrates 5.8g; Protein 27.3g

Tilapia

Serving Size: 4

Cooking Time: 20 minutes

Ingredients:

- ¼ teaspoon sea salt
- 1 sliced avocado
- 1 tablespoons fresh orange juice
- also needed: 9-inch pie plate
- four 4 oz. - more rectangular than square tilapia fillets
- 1 tablespoon olive oil
- ¼ cup red onion

Directions:

1. Combine the salt, juice, and oil to add to the pie dish. Work with one fillet at a time. Place it in the dish and turn to coat all sides.
2. Arrange the fillets in a wagon wheel-shaped formation. (Each of the fillets should be in the center of the dish with the other end draped over the edge.)
3. Place a tbsp of the onion on top of each fillet and fold the end into the center.
4. Place in the microwave using the high heat setting for three minutes. It's done when the center can be easily flaked.
5. Top the fillets off with avocado and serve.

Nutritional Value: Calories 200; Fat 11g; Carbohydrates 31g; Protein 22g

Poultry and Meat Recipes

Artichoke Beef Roast

Serving Size: 6

Cooking Time: 45 minutes

Ingredients:

- 2 lbs beef roast, cubed
- 1 tablespoon garlic, minced
- 1 onion, chopped
- 1/2 teaspoon paprika
- 1 tablespoon parsley, chopped
- 2 tomatoes, chopped
- 1 tablespoon capers, chopped
- 10 oz can artichokes, drained and chopped
- 2 cups chicken stock
- 1 tablespoon olive oil
- Pepper
- Salt

Directions:

1. Oil and heat the pot, add onions and garlic.
2. Add meat and cook until brown.
3. Add remaining ingredients and stir well.
4. Once done, allow to release pressure naturally. Remove lid.
5. Serve and enjoy.

Nutritional Value: Calories 344; Fat 12.2g; Carbohydrates 9.2g; Protein 48.4g

Chicken and Artichokes

Serving Size: 4

Cooking Time: 30 minutes

Ingredients:

- 2 pounds of chicken breast, skinless, boneless, and sliced
- A pinch of salt and black pepper
- 4 tablespoons of olive oil
- 8 ounces of canned roasted artichoke hearts, drained
- 6 ounces of sun-dried tomatoes, chopped
- 3 tablespoons of capers, drained
- 2 tablespoons of lemon juice

Directions:

1. Oil and heat the pan add the artichokes and the other ingredients except the chicken, stir and sauté for 10 minutes.
2. Transfer the mix to a bowl, heat up the pan again with the rest of the oil over medium-high heat temperature, add the meat and cook for 4 minutes on each side.
3. Return the veggie mix to the pan, toss, cook everything for 2-3 minutes more, divide between plates, and serve.

Nutritional Value: Calories 452; Fat 28g; Carbohydrates 33g; Protein 43g

Ground Pork Skillet

Serving Size: 6

Cooking Time: 25 minutes

Ingredients:

- 2 1/4 pounds ground pork
- 3 tablespoons olive oil
- 1 1/2 bunch kale, trimmed and roughly chopped
- 1 1/2 cup onions, sliced
- 1/3 teaspoon black pepper, or more to taste
- 1/3 cup tomato puree
- 1 1/2 bell pepper, chopped
- 1 1/2 teaspoon sea salt
- 1 1/2 cup chicken bone broth
- 1/3 cup port wine
- 3/4 cloves garlic, pressed
- 1 1/2 chili pepper, sliced

Directions:

1. Oil and heat the pan to cook the garlic, onion and peppers until soft and aromatic; set aside.
2. Cook the ground pork for 5 minutes, or until no longer pink, in the remaining tablespoon of olive oil.
3. Cook for 15 to 17 minutes, or until the other ingredients are cooked thoroughly.
4. Storing
5. Defrost in the refrigerator. Enjoy!

Nutritional Value: Calories 349; Fat 13g; Carbohydrates 4.4g; Protein 45.3g

Herb and Pistachio Turkey Breasts

Serving Size: 4

Cooking Time: 50 minutes

Ingredients:

- ½ cup of pistachios, toasted and chopped
- 1 tablespoon of olive oil
- 1 pound of turkey breast, cubed
- 1 cup of chicken stock
- 1 tablespoon of basil, chopped
- 1 tablespoon of rosemary, chopped
- 1 tablespoon of oregano, chopped
- 1 tablespoon of parsley, chopped
- 1 tablespoon of tarragon, chopped
- 3 garlic cloves, minced
- 3 cups of tomatoes, chopped

Directions:

1. Warm the olive oil in a large-sized skillet over medium heat and cook turkey and garlic for 5 minutes.
2. Stir in stock, basil, rosemary, oregano, parsley, tarragon, pistachios, and tomatoes and bring to a simmer. Cook for 35 minutes. Serve immediately.

Nutritional Value: Calories 310; Fat 12g; Carbohydrates 20g; Protein 25g

Pot-Roast Veal

Serving Size: 8

Cooking Time: 5 hours

Ingredients:

- 2 tablespoons olive oil
- Salt and pepper
- 1 cup chicken or veal stock
- 3-pound boneless veal roast, tied
- 4 medium carrots, peeled
- 2 parsnips, peeled and halved
- 2 white turnips, peeled and quartered
- 10 garlic cloves, peeled
- 2 sprigs of fresh thyme
- 1 orange, scrubbed and zested

Directions:

1. Oil and heat the pan, Scour veal roast all over with olive oil, then season with salt and pepper. Once hot, situate the veal roast and sear on all sides. This will take about 3 minutes on every side, but this process seals in the juices and makes the meat succulent.
2. When cooked, place it in the slow cooker. Throw in the carrots, parsnips, turnips, and garlic into the skillet. Cook for 5 minutes.
3. Situate vegetables in the slow cooker, placing them all around the meat. Top the roast with the thyme and the zest from the orange. Slice the orange into 2 and squeeze the juice over the top of the meat. Fill in chicken stock, then cook the roast on low for 5 hours.

Nutritional Value: Calories 252; Fat 12g; Carbohydrates 10g; Protein 48g

Sides, Salads and Soup Recipes

Baked Tomato

Serving Size: 4

Cooking Time: 25 minutes

Ingredients:

- Whole grain bread
- Salt and pepper to taste
- 1 tbsp. of finely chopped basil
- 2 cloves of garlic. Finely chopped
- Extra virgin oil
- 2 large tomatoes

Directions:

1. Preheat your oven to 400°F.
2. Use the olive oil to brush the bottom of a baking dish. Set aside.
3. Slice the tomatoes into a thickness of ½ inch. Lay the tomato pieces into the baking dish that you had prepared earlier.
4. Bake for about 20-25 minutes. Serve and enjoy.

Nutritional Value: Calories 342; Fat 10g; Carbohydrates 45g; Protein 16g

Balsamic Beets

Serving Size: 6

Cooking Time: 30 minutes

Ingredients:

- 3 medium beets, sliced
- 1/3 cup balsamic vinegar
- 1 teaspoon rosemary, chopped
- 1 garlic clove, minced
- ½ teaspoon Italian seasoning
- A drizzle of olive oil

Directions:

1. In a bowl, mix rosemary with vinegar, garlic, Italian seasoning, and the beets, toss and leave aside for 10 minutes.
2. Place beets and the marinade on aluminum foil pieces, add a drizzle of oil, seal edges, place on a preheated grill pan over medium heat, and cook for 25 minutes.
3. Unwrap beets, peel, cube them, divide between plates and serve as a side dish.

Nutritional Value: Calories 100; Fat 2g; Carbohydrates 2g; Protein 4g

Carrot and Broccoli Salad

Serving Size: 4

Cooking Time: 15 minutes

Ingredients:

- 8 ounces of whole-wheat pasta
- 2 cups of broccoli florets
- 1 cup of peeled and shredded carrots
- ¼ cup of plain Greek yogurt
- Juice of 1 lemon
- 1 teaspoon of red pepper flakes
- Salt and ground pepper, to taste

Directions:

1. Boil water and add the pasta. Drain the pasta and let rest for a few minutes.
2. When cooled, combine the pasta with the veggies, yogurt, lemon juice, and red pepper flakes in a large-sized bowl, and stir thoroughly to combine. Serve immediately.

Nutritional Value: Calories 428; Fat 2.9g; Carbohydrates 84.6g; Protein 15.9g

Chicken Kale Wraps

Serving Size: 4

Cooking Time: 10 minutes

Ingredients:

- 1 tablespoon of mayonnaise
- 1 teaspoon of Dijon mustard
- 3 medium kale leaves
- 3 ounces of cooked chicken breast, sliced
- 6 thin red onion slices
- 1 firm apple, cut into 9 slices

Directions:

1. Mix the mustard with mayonnaise in a small bowl.
2. Spread the kale leaves onto the serving platter.
3. Top the leaves with an even layer of mayo mixture.
4. Place 1 ounces of chicken, 2 onion slices and 3 slices of apple on top of each leave.
5. Roll the leaves to wrap the veggies.
6. Cut each roll in half and serve.

Nutritional Value: Calories 216; Fat 4.4g; Carbohydrates 38.9g; Protein 9.5g

Creamy Carrot Chowder

Serving Size: 8

Cooking Time: 40 minutes

Ingredients:

- 8 fresh mint sprigs
- ½ cup 2% Greek Style Plain yogurt
- 1 teaspoon fresh ginger
- 2 cups chicken broth
- 1 pound of baby carrots
- 1/3 cup sliced shallots
- 2 teaspoons sesame oil

Directions:

1. On medium fire, place a medium heavy bottom pot and heat oil.
2. Sauté shallots until tender around minutes.
3. Add carrots and sauté for another 4 minutes.
4. Pour broth, cover, and bring to a boil once the soup is boiling, slow fire to a simmer, and cook carrots until tender for 22 minutes.
5. Add ginger and continue cooking while covered for another eight minutes.
6. Turn off the heat and cool for 10 minutes.
7. Pour mixture into blender and puree. If needed, puree carrots in batches, then return to pot.
8. Heat pureed carrots until heated through around 2 minutes.
9. Turn off the fire and evenly pour into 8 serving bowls.
10. Serve.

Nutritional Value: Calories 147; Fat 1.6g; Carbohydrates 14g; Protein 2.2g

Crispy Sweet Potato Fries

Serving Size: 4

Cooking Time: 10 minutes

Ingredients:

- 1 1/2 lbs. sweet potatoes
- Sea salt
- Garlic powder
- Onion powder

Directions:

1. In a cast-iron skillet over medium-high to high heat, add 1/2 to 1 inch of oil.
2. When the oil is hot, and you can begin to see little air pockets forming, add the sweet potato fries to the container.
3. Fry until they are brilliant darker, and marginally firm, around 10 minutes.
4. Remove from oil and move to a paper towel to absorb excess oil.
5. Add sea salt, garlic powder, and onion powder in a little bowl. Sprinkle flavoring over top of the sweet potato fries.

Nutritional Value: Calories 102; Fat 8g; Carbohydrates 23.7g; Protein 4g

Endive Salad

Serving Size: 4

Cooking Time: 10 minutes

Ingredients:

- 1 tablespoon of lemon juice
- 1 tablespoon of balsamic vinegar
- 2 pears, sliced lengthwise
- 1 teaspoon of Dijon mustard
- Sea salt and pepper to taste
- 12 black olives, chopped
- 1 tablespoon of parsley, chopped
- 2 tablespoons of olive oil
- 7 cups of baby spinach
- 2 endives, shredded
- 2 garlic cloves, minced
- 2 bulbs of fennel, shredded

Directions:

1. Place spinach, endives, pears, fennel, parsley, olives, salt, pepper, lemon juice, olive oil, mustard, garlic, and balsamic vinegar in a medium-sized bowl and toss to combine.
2. Serve right away.

Nutritional Value: Calories 100; Fat 10g; Carbohydrates 4g; Protein 2g

Leeks Soup

Serving Size: 6

Cooking Time: 1 hour 25 minutes

Ingredients:

- 2 gold potatoes, chopped
- 1 cup of cauliflower florets
- Black pepper to the taste
- 5 leeks, chopped
- 4 garlic cloves, minced
- 1 yellow onion, chopped
- 3 tablespoons of olive oil
- A handful of parsley, chopped
- 4 cups of low-sodium chicken stock

Directions:

1. Oil and heat the pan, add onion and garlic, stir, and cook for 5 minutes.
2. Add potatoes, cauliflower, black pepper, leeks, and stock, stir, bring to a simmer, cook over medium heat for 30 minutes, blend using an immersion blender, add parsley, stir, ladle into bowls, and serve.

Nutritional Value: Calories 150; Fat 8g; Carbohydrates 7g; Protein 8g

Mushroom Spinach Soup

Serving Size: 4

Cooking Time: 25 minutes

Ingredients:

- 1 cup of spinach, cleaned and chopped
- 100 grams of mushrooms, chopped
- 1 onion
- 6 garlic cloves
- ½ teaspoon of red chili powder
- Salt and black pepper, to taste
- 3 tablespoons of buttermilk
- 1 teaspoon of almond flour
- 2 cups of chicken broth
- 3 tablespoons of butter
- ¼ cup of fresh cream for garnish

Directions:

1. Oil and heat the pan to cook the garlic and onions cook for 5 minutes and add salt, spinach, and red chili powder. Sauté for about 4 minutes and add mushrooms.
2. Blend puree.
3. Return to the pan and add buttermilk and almond flour for a creamy texture.
4. Mix well and simmer for about 2 minutes.
5. Serve hot.

Nutritional Value: Calories 160; Fat 13.3g; Carbohydrates 7g; Protein 4.7g

White Bean and Kale Soup with Chicken

Serving Size: 6

Cooking Time: 30 minutes

Ingredients:

- Sea salt + black pepper
- 3 cups kale
- 1 15-oz can white beans
- 2 cups chicken
- 1 strip bacon
- 4 cloves garlic
- 8 cups broth
- 1 cup white onion
- 1 tablespoon avocado oil

Directions:

1. Oil and heat the skillet to cook the onions.
2. Then add garlic and cook for another 2-3 minutes. Carry to a boil the broth, completely soaked white beans and meat.
3. To blend the flavors, cook for ten minutes. After that, sprinkle with salt and pepper. add the kale. Serve instantly.

Nutritional Value: Calories 280; Fat 12.1g; Carbohydrates 7.4g; Protein 34g

Dessert Recipes

Blueberry Muffins

Serving Size: 4

Cooking Time: 25 minutes

Ingredients:

- 1 cup whole wheat flour
- 1 teaspoon baking powder
- ¼ cup blueberries
- 1 teaspoon vanilla extract
- 1 tablespoon butter softened
- ¾ cup sour cream
- 1 tablespoon Erythritol
- Cooking spray

Directions:

1. In the mixing bowl, combine wheat flour and baking powder.
2. Then add sour cream, vanilla extract, butter, and Erythritol.
3. Stir the mixture well until smooth. You should get a thick batter. Add more sour cream if needed.
4. After this, add blueberries and carefully stir the batter.
5. Spray the muffin molds with the cooking spray.
6. Fill ½ part of every muffin mold with batter.
7. Preheat the oven to 365F.
8. Place the muffins in the prepared oven and cook them for 25 minutes.
9. The cooked muffins will have a golden color surface.

Nutritional Value: Calories 241; Fat 12.4g; Carbohydrates 24.9g; Protein 1.9g

Cherry Clafoutis

Serving Size: 6

Cooking Time: 1 hour

Ingredients:

- 1 ¼ pounds of sweet cherries
- 3 large eggs
- ½ cup of all-purpose flour
- 1 teaspoon of vanilla extract
- 1/8 teaspoon of almond extract
- ½ cup and 3 tablespoons of sugar
- 1 ⅓ cup of whole milk
- Softened butter, for the baking dish

Directions:

1. Preheat your oven at 375°F. Grease a 2 quarts of baking dish with butter. Spread the pitted cherries onto the baking dish.
2. Blend the ingredients, flour and eggs until smooth. Bake for 45 minutes. Serve.

Nutritional Value: Calories 352; Fat 15g; Carbohydrates 51g; Protein 34g

Citrus Ciambella

Serving Size: 10

Cooking Time: 35 minutes

Ingredients:

- 1 ½ cups granulated sugar
- 1 tablespoon lemon zest
- ½ cup lemon juice
- 5 large eggs
- ½ cup light-tasting olive oil
- 2 cups all-purpose flour
- 2 teaspoons baking powder
- ½ teaspoon salt
- Confectioners' sugar (optional)
- Nonstick cooking spray

Directions:

1. Mix the eggs sugar, and zest.
2. Mix in the lemon juice and oil.
3. Add the baking powder, flour, and salt. Combine well.
4. Pour the already prepared batter into the prepared pan and bake for 35–40 minutes until a toothpick inserted comes out clean.
5. Dust with confectioners' sugar (if using).

Nutritional Value: Calories 264; Fat 15g; Carbohydrates 30g; Protein 2g

Cocoa Brownies

Serving Size: 8

Cooking Time: 30 minutes

Ingredients:

- 30 ounces of canned lentils, rinsed and drained
- 1 tablespoon of honey
- 1 banana, peeled and chopped
- ½ teaspoon of baking soda
- 4 tablespoons of almond butter
- 2 tablespoons of cocoa powder
- Cooking spray

Directions:

1. Preheat the oven to 375°F.
2. In a food processor, combine the lentils with the honey and the other ingredients except for the cooking spray and pulse well.
3. Pour the mixture into a medium-sized pan greased with the cooking spray, making sure to spread the mixture out evenly.
4. Cut the brownies and serve cold.

Nutritional Value: Calories 200; Fat 4.5g; Carbohydrates 8.7g; Protein 4.3g

Fig and Honey Buckwheat Pudding

Serving Size: 4

Cooking Time: 10 minutes

Ingredients:

- 1/2 teaspoon ground cinnamon
- 1/2 cup dried figs, chopped
- 1/3 cup honey
- 1 teaspoon pure vanilla extract
- 3 ½ cups milk
- 1/2 teaspoon pure almond extract
- 1 ½ cups buckwheat

Directions:

1. Mix all the ingredients in a pot.
2. Secure the lid. Choose the "Multigrain" mode and cook for 10 minutes under high pressure.
3. Serve topped with fresh fruits, nuts, or whipped topping. Bon appétit!

Nutritional Value: Calories 320; Fat 7.5g; Carbohydrates 57.7g; Protein 9.5g

Maple Baked Pears

Serving Size: 4

Cooking Time: 35 minutes

Ingredients:

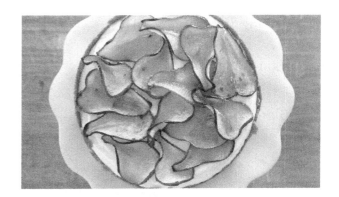

- 4 Anjou pears, halved and cored
- ¼ teaspoon of ground cinnamon
- ½ cup of pure maple syrup
- 1 teaspoon of pure vanilla extract

Directions:

1. Arrange the pear halves onto the prepared baking sheet, cut side upwards, and sprinkle with cinnamon.
2. In a small bowl, add the vanilla syrup, maple syrup and beat well.
3. Reserve about 2 tablespoons of the maple syrup mixture.
4. Place the remaining maple syrup mixture over the pears and bake for 25 minutes or until lightly browned.
5. Remove from the preheated oven and immediately drizzle with the reserved maple syrup mixture. Serve warm.

Nutritional Value: Calories 227; Fat 4g; Carbohydrates 58.5g; Protein 1g

Rose Crème Caramel

Serving Size: 2

Cooking Time: 35 minutes

Ingredients:

- 2 eggs
- 1 cup of low fat cream
- 1 cup of milk
- 2 tablespoons of sugar
- 1 tablespoon of rose syrup
- Caramel syrup
- 2 tablespoons of sugar
- 2 tablespoons of water

Directions:

1. Mix the tablespoons of water and sugar in a saucepan and cook until it caramelizes, stirring occasionally. Divide the caramel into 4 ramekins. Preheat your oven at 350°F.
2. In a bowl, beat the eggs with rose syrup, sugar, cream and milk. Divide this mixture into the ramekins then bake for 25 minutes. Allow the crème caramel to cool then refrigerate for 6 hours. Run a knife around the dessert and flip onto a serving plate. Serve.

Nutritional Value: Calories 358; Fat 20.8g; Carbohydrates 31.9g; Protein 13.1g

Spanish Nougat

Serving Size: 12

Cooking Time: 32 minutes

Ingredients:

- 1 1/2 cup of honey
- 3 egg whites
- 1 ¾ cup of almonds, toasted and chopped

Directions:

1. Boil the honey and let it cool. Beat the egg whites to a thick glossy meringue and fold them into the honey.
2. When the color and consistency change to a dark caramel, remove from heat, add the almonds and mix through. Pour the heated mixture into a 9x13 inch pan lined with foil. Cover with another piece of foil and even out. Let cool completely. Place a wooden board weighted down with some heavy cans on it. Leave like this for 3-4 days, so it hardens and dries out. Slice into 1-inch squares.

Nutritional Value: Calories 189; Fat 12g; Carbohydrates 29.1g; Protein 5.8g

Vanilla Bread Pudding with Apricots

Serving Size: 6

Cooking Time: 15 minutes

Ingredients:

- 2 tablespoons coconut oil
- 1 1/3 cups heavy cream
- 4 eggs, whisked
- 1/2 cup dried apricots, soaked and chopped
- 1 teaspoon cinnamon, ground
- 1/2 teaspoon star anise, ground
- A pinch of grated nutmeg
- A pinch of salt
- 1/2 cup granulated sugar
- 2 tablespoons molasses
- 2 cups milk
- 4 cups Italian bread, cubed
- 1 teaspoon vanilla paste

Directions:

1. Add 1 ½ cups of water and a metal rack to the Instant Pot.
2. Grease a baking dish with a nonstick cooking spray. Throw the bread cubes into the prepared baking dish.
3. In a mixing bowl, thoroughly combine the remaining ingredients.
4. Once cooking is complete, use a quick pressure release; carefully remove the lid. Enjoy!

Nutritional Value: Calories 410; Fat 24.3g; Carbohydrates 37.4g; Protein 11.5g

White Chocolate Brie Cups

Serving Size: 15

Cooking Time: 25 minutes

Ingredients:

- 1/3 cup orange marmalade
- Kumquat slices
- 1 ounce's white chocolate
- 2 ounces Brie cheese
- 1 package phyllo tart shells

Directions:

1. Fill each tart casing halfway with chocolate, then halfway with cheddar.
2. Place on a cookie dish that hasn't been buttered. Serve with a dollop of marmalade on top.
3. Preheat oven to 375°F and bake until lightly browned.
4. Warm the dish before serving. Kumquats may be added on the top if desired.

Nutritional Value: Calories 236; Fat 2g; Carbohydrates 17.4g; Protein 4.5g

30-Day Meal Plan

Day	Breakfast	Lunch	Dinner
1	Cheesy Green Bites	Tilapia with Avocado and Red Onion	Eggplant Ratatouille
2	Omelet	Herb and Pistachio Turkey Breasts	Seafood Gumbo
3	Stuffed Pita Breads	Chicken Curry Rice	Ground Pork Skillet
4	Poaches Eggs with Avocado Puree	Shrimp Zoodles	Chicken and Artichokes
5	Artichoke Frittata	Brown Rice Pilaf with Pistachios and Raisins	Turkey Pasta Toss
6	Heavenly Egg Bake with Blackberry	Cauliflower Curry	Broiled Salmon
7	Buttery Pancakes	Chicken and Artichokes	Pot-Roast Veal
8	Tuna Breakfast Quiche	Ground Pork Skillet	Asparagus Risotto
9	Stuffed Pita Breads	Eggplant Ratatouille	Artichokes Provencal
10	Avocado Baked Eggs	Seafood Gumbo	Broiled Salmon
11	Cheesy Green Bites	Asparagus Risotto	Chicken Curry Rice

12	Omelet	Zucchini Lasagna Rolls	Artichoke Beef Roast
13	Artichoke Frittata	Brown Rice Pilaf with Pistachios and Raisins	Zucchini Lasagna Rolls
14	Heavenly Egg Bake with Blackberry	Pot-Roast Veal	Veggie Quesadillas
15	Nectarin Bruschetta	Broiled Salmon	Brown Rice Pilad with Pistachios and Raisins
16	Stuffed Pita Breads	Chicken and Artichokes	Shrimp Zoodles
17	Buttery Pancakes	Chicken Curry Rice	Ground Pork Skillet
18	Artichoke Frittata	Brown Rice Pilad with Pistachios and Raisins	Eggplant Ratatouille
19	Tuna Breakfast Quiche	Artichokes Provencal	Artichoke Beef Roast
20	Omelet	Shrimp Zoodles	Asparagus Risotto
21	Poached Eggs with Avocado Puree	Ground Pork Skillet	Seafood Gumbo
22	Artichoke Frittata	Turkey Pasta Toss	Mushroom Risotto
23	Heavenly Egg Bake with Blackberry	Eggplant Ratatouille	Cauliflower Curry
24	Cheesy Green Bites	Halibut with Kale	Artichokes Provencal

25	Avocado Baked Eggs	Herb and Pistachio Turkey Breasts	Broiles Salmon
26	Buttery Pancakes	Seafood Gumbo	Chicken and Artichokes
27	Tuna Breakfast Quiche	Cauliflower Curry	Halibut with Kale
28	Nectatin Bruschetta	Artichoke Beef Roast	Brown Rice Pilad with Pistachios and Raisins
29	Omelet	Shrimp Zoodles	Zucchini Lasagna Rolls
30	Poached Eggs with Avocado Puree	Eggplant Ratatouille	Chicken Curry Rice

Conclusion

Thank you for the time to read The Mediterranean Diet. I expect that it provided you with a well-rounded understanding of the Mediterranean diet and everything it encompasses. This will honestly give all of you a diverse meal plan that will be flavorful and healthy at the same time. Unfortunately, it is challenging to find great-tasting food that is also good for you. Furthermore, much of the health food out there is anything but this. Juices that claim to be healthy are loaded with sugar. Meals that claim to have hearty ingredients with fillers and way too much salt.

With the Mediterranean diet, this will not be of concern. If you follow the traditional meal plans with authentic ingredients, we all but guarantee delicious food that will have tremendous health benefits, give you extra energy, and help you prevent many chronic illnesses.

In addition to understanding the Mediterranean diet, we hope you will fully incorporate it into your lives by following the many recipe plans in this book. These will provide a base for your cooking and allow you to create your delicious meal ideas as an offshoot. Just be mindful of the ingredients that you use because they are what determine whether your meal is healthy or not.

I want you to succeed and advise you also to try the 7-day plan. Feel free to create your variations, as the one I provided is only meant to be used as an example. In the end, I want you to experience a healthy and life-changing diet each day. If you enjoyed this book, I hope you will share the information with any of your friends and family, as it is much more fun to break bread with those you love. The Mediterranean diet is the healthiest diet available, and I urge as many people as possible to try it.

Made in the USA
Las Vegas, NV
01 April 2023